M. Mitrović   M. Schuster

Hiking Meteora Monasteries

Explore the most popular routes to the monasteries

Bibliografische Information der Deutschen Nationalbibliothek:
Die Deutsche Nationalbibliothek verzeichnet diese Publikation
in der Deutschen Nationalbibliografie;
detaillierte bibliografische Daten sind im Internet über
dnb.dnb.de abrufbar.

Herstellung und Verlag:
BoD – Books on Demand, Norderstedt
ISBN: 978-3-7578-1727-5

Content

Egyptian vulture – Neophron percnopterus

Prologue

The region of Meteora Monasteries belongs to the World Cultural Heritage. Unlike on the Holy Mountain of Athos, here female and male tourists have a unique opportunity to dive deeply into the essence of the Orthodox religion. And similarly to the monastic republic on the Halkidiki peninsula, which is accessible only to men, the religious life of the Meteora Monasteries receives its special charm from the scenic ambience with its memorable rock formations. In fact, the first monks who settled here were looking for or were attracted by just such magical landscapes. So there is an interaction between spiritual inspiration and the magic of the place.

It is therefore all the more surprising that the vast majority of visitors arrive in motor vehicles and drive as far as possible to the desired monastery, including young, healthy, sporty people. They do this because of a lack of time or may be they are unaware of the many hiking possibilities. They are also afraid of the heat, and last but not least because they generally avoid exertion.

With our hiking guide, we would like to encourage and inspire all nature lovers to explore the beautiful and spectacular region in the most natural way, just as the monks did for centuries: on foot! We have selected eight routes around the monasteries, added one to the neighboring villages and a tour of Kalabaka.

All start and end in the center of Kalabaka. You can alternatively take the bus or your own car to cover parts of the route. All eight hiking routes are almost exclusively off the asphalt roads, all paths do not require climbing skills or equipment. Good footwear goes without saying. Provisions should be taken with you, there are canteen cars only at the big monasteries, otherwise you have to rely on yourself. From all routes you can quickly reach the road and in case of emergency you can go back by bus.

The best season for hiking in Thessaly is from mid-March to mid-May and from mid-September to mid-November. In spring it is not yet so hot, there is still snow on the distant mountains and the streams drain their water into the Pinios. If you don't like hustle and bustle, you should not come for the Orthodox Easter. On the other hand, this is just a good opportunity to get acquainted with the religious customs. In autumn it is often still very warm during the day, but it gets cool at night. The weather is unstable, it can rain for a few hours. In summer it is very hot, then hiking tours with a high proportion of forest and an early morning start are recommended. If you hike in the sun, you must protect yourself well and drink about one liter per hour.

A conscious decision was made not to go into detail about the history and culture of the region and the

Varlaam Monastery

monasteries. On the one hand, this would go beyond the scope of a handy guide and would decisively shift the thematic weight. On the other hand, there is enough literature to buy in the monasteries and souvenir stores in town, also in English. Some notes are added now and then in the text.

By way of introduction, the currently most probable geological history of the formation of this mystical looking rock formation is briefly explained.

All important practical information is available in Kalabaka: in all hotels and guesthouses the free leaflet 'Meteora maps' is available, there are also several travel agencies and tourist information offices where you can book guided tours, e.g. half-day hiking tours or 'sunset' bus tours etc.

There are just two ways to approach this unique world: to come for hiking out of interest in the monasteries - or to discover the monasteries while hiking! The author of these lines has taken the first way and then searched, found and walked the whole network of paths and trails. Because this should be immediately clear to every visitor of the Meteora area: a single visit is not enough to feel and understand the magic of the place!

Brief introduction to the geology of Meteora

Seen from close up, they look as if the gods had built them out of cement and gravel, which also corresponds to the mythical story of the origin of the rocks of Meteora.

Some of the stone pillars rise more than three hundred meters into the sky, covered by a green roof of willows and meadows, on which the monasteries are majestically enthroned. Their full beauty unfolds from a distance, especially under the influence of the interactions between weather and sunlight. Sometimes they rise cool and gray from the morning mist, sometimes they shine in the golden light of the evening sun. This unique cultural and landscape ensemble unfolds its charms at any time of day or year. And it is easy for the visitor to understand why the monks from the 13th century onwards built their monasteries here, which were almost inaccessible until the 20th century.

In addition to the mythical origin story, there is, of course, also a geological one or more.

However, we want to limit ourselves here to the most plausible explanation, which is largely based on the German-Jewish geographer and geologist Alfred Philippson (1864 - 1953), who visited the region around Kalabaka, Kastraki and Meteora in 1893 and published his travel reports and research results in 1897 in his work 'Thessaly and Epirus'.

The formation history of the rock towers, which are solitary in this region, dates back about 30 million years to the Oligocene in the late Paleogene.

At that time, an Oligocene estuary extended where the Pinios River now runs, and calcareous sediments were deposited there over time.

A tectonic uplift began that lasted for several million years. About 23 million years ago, a river coming from the northeast flowed into the sea. In the course of time, a large amount of rocks and boulders, as well as sandy and muddy sediment, had been deposited in the river delta.

The meteoric rocks consist of this sedimentary conglomerate formed under pressure, of pebbles of different types of sedimentary, metamorphic and volcanic rocks of earlier epochs, rounded by friction, and are enveloped by sandstone.

This assumption is also confirmed by the fact that the rocks of the conglomerate are completely different from those of the Pindos Mountains, which today lie on the opposite side of the river.

The uplift and draining of the delta created tectonic fractures in the conglomerate rock. The subsequent forces of erosion by water, wind, ice and earthquakes especially along these fault lines eventually carved out the present rock formations of Meteora, while the eroded material below was deposited around the rocks or transported away.

1. Hiking route: Around St. Stephen's Mountain (Agia Triada and Agios Stefanos)

On this hike we have the opportunity to visit two monasteries. It goes through dense mixed forest, over meadows as well as through a gorge. The pure hiking time is about two hours, with breaks and visit of a monastery 3 ½ to 4 hours. We start at the 'Town Hall Square' (Δημαρχειο) and walk up the Vlachava Street. On the left we see the church of St. Vissarion ❶, on whose dome storks nest from spring to September. Nearby, up a side street (Odos Fidou), is the small church of St. John the Baptist, built before 1336. Also there nearby (Odos Nikis) is the church of Saint Barbara, built in 1798.

At the end of the street, it turns into Canarias Street and shortly after, the actual footpath begins, which is advertised as 40 minutes to the monastery of Agia Triada. Most of the path is paved with cobblestones, it is impossible to get lost. From ever new vantage points we look down to Kalabaka, up into the surrounding rocky world or to the monastery of Agia Triada. Some particularly beautiful spots invite us to linger ❷. The green aisles between the rock formations to the left, leading up to the spindle on the Kastrakis side, are no problem for experienced climbers. At the top we have the possibility to go to the right to the monastery of Agia Triada ❸, from whose advanced rock plateau we can enjoy a breathtaking view of Kalabaka and its hinterland. The church, with its iconostasis and murals, is worth seeing.

Turn right up to the asphalt road and continue on it to the monastery of Agios Stefanos ❹. It is only a few hundred meters to this large nunnery. Unfortunately, the hiking trail from there to the north around the mountain of St. Stephen has been blocked, so you have to go back the same way on the road.

If we turn left at the asphalt road, after 200 meters we arrive at a proskinitario (image of a saint with a cottage) ❺ on the right side of the road. It invites you to take a short rest. Sometimes cows run along the road, having escaped from the nearby pasture in the Agias Trias valley. At Proskinitario we turn right up the mountain of St. Stephen, the path is wide and goes along the gorge below the mountain. At the bottom we see pastures and dilapidated shepherd's huts.

At a sharp bend to the right, we turn left onto a footpath downhill that leads us through a beautiful deciduous forest in gentle switchbacks down to the chapel of Analepsis ❻. The direction of the walk is initially northwest, then mainly east and southeast. The chapel is an unadorned new building, a bench in front of it invites you to rest.

Passing the chapel, the path now leads across meadows onto a paved path, which we leave shortly after the

Agia Triada Monastery with a view of Kalabaka
Agios Stefanos Monastery
Theopetra Rock, Trikala in the background

first houses to turn right. We cross an old sand pit ❼, descend a meadow and finally come out at Analipseos road, which we follow to a larger square. On the way we pass the military cemetery ❽ where victims of the Greek Civil War rest.

Unfortunately, the cemetery is only accessible on Ochi Day. We turn into Rammidi Street and along it we return to the center of Kalabaka.

Wine press - Monastery of Great Meteoron

500m

Rousanou

5

N

3
Agia Triada

2

6

Spindle

Agios Stefanos
4

7

8

1

Kalabaka

2. Hiking route: Via the Cat Church to the great monasteries and back (Agios Rousanou, Agios Varlaam, Agios Metamorfosis, Agios Nikolaos)

On this route we climb through several gorges, cross ancient forests and have the opportunity to visit two monasteries. The way back leads us through the neighbouring village of Kastraki. It takes about 3 hours without visiting a monastery. From the centre of Kalabaka we walk the same way as on the first route until shortly after the beginning of the paved ascent to the monastery of Agia Triada. At a large boulder ❶ our path branches off to the left up the rock, which is also signposted (inscription on the rock). Only the first few metres are a bit strenuous and require surefootedness, after that it becomes easier. As we climb, we get closer to the Alyssos wall on the left, sometimes you can watch a small herd of goats at breakneck points. At various places, the shepherds set up water buckets for the animals to drink.

Eventually we get tight between Modi and Delta Wall ❷, a popular spot for climbing beginners. There are several small routes for beginners on the not very high rock, their local knowledgeable guides take care that nothing happens. At the top, we keep to the right on the path until we reach the junction. Straight ahead

Cat Church
Fire salamander
Kastraki with Holy Spirit Rock

we go in a big curve to the monastery of Agia Triada. We turn left down through a beautiful deciduous forest. In high summer it is refreshingly cool here, in the dim late autumn it is quite gloomy! In rainy weather we can often see fire salamanders on the paths.

We reach the asphalt road from Kastraki ❸ to the higher monasteries. On the right, after three hundred metres, we reach the nunnery of Rousanou. We choose the path down to the left - unfortunately about 400m along the road. At a sharp left turn we leave the road and turn right, up into the Plakes Arsaniotikes, a gently rising valley dominated in the middle by a rocky outcrop, the Cat Church ❹. In winter, a lively stream gurgles here, but towards the end of March, almost all the streams in the Meteora area have dried up. Stone markers show us the way, which is easy to lose, especially above the Cat Church.

We now reach the road to the monasteries of Varlaam and Metamorfosis. On the grounds of Varlaam Monastery ❺, we turn right onto the sloping path to the monastery garden. It leads us out of the monastery grounds (the old gate is no longer closed at sunset, as it used to be!) and down a mostly well-surfaced path to the road coming from Kastraki. The turn-off to the right just below the gate leads to the monastery of Metamorfosis. At this point we can admire ancient tree giants, whose partly dead parts make mighty circumferences. Halfway up, a small footpath on the left leads up to the Dragon's Cave ❻, a spacious overhang that can be seen from far away.

We cross the road and walk downhill on a stony path through bushes and trees. To the left above us on the wall of the Holy Spirit Rock, we see the colourful flags brought up there by young men at the abandoned monastery of St. George ❼ every year on 23 April, the saint's day.

We pass through the village of Kastraki, which we will visit in more detail on another occasion. Now we want to walk along the main road back to Kalabaka. At the restaurant 'Panorama' ❽ we turn left and shorten the distance.

Monk skulls – Monastery of Great Meteoron

21

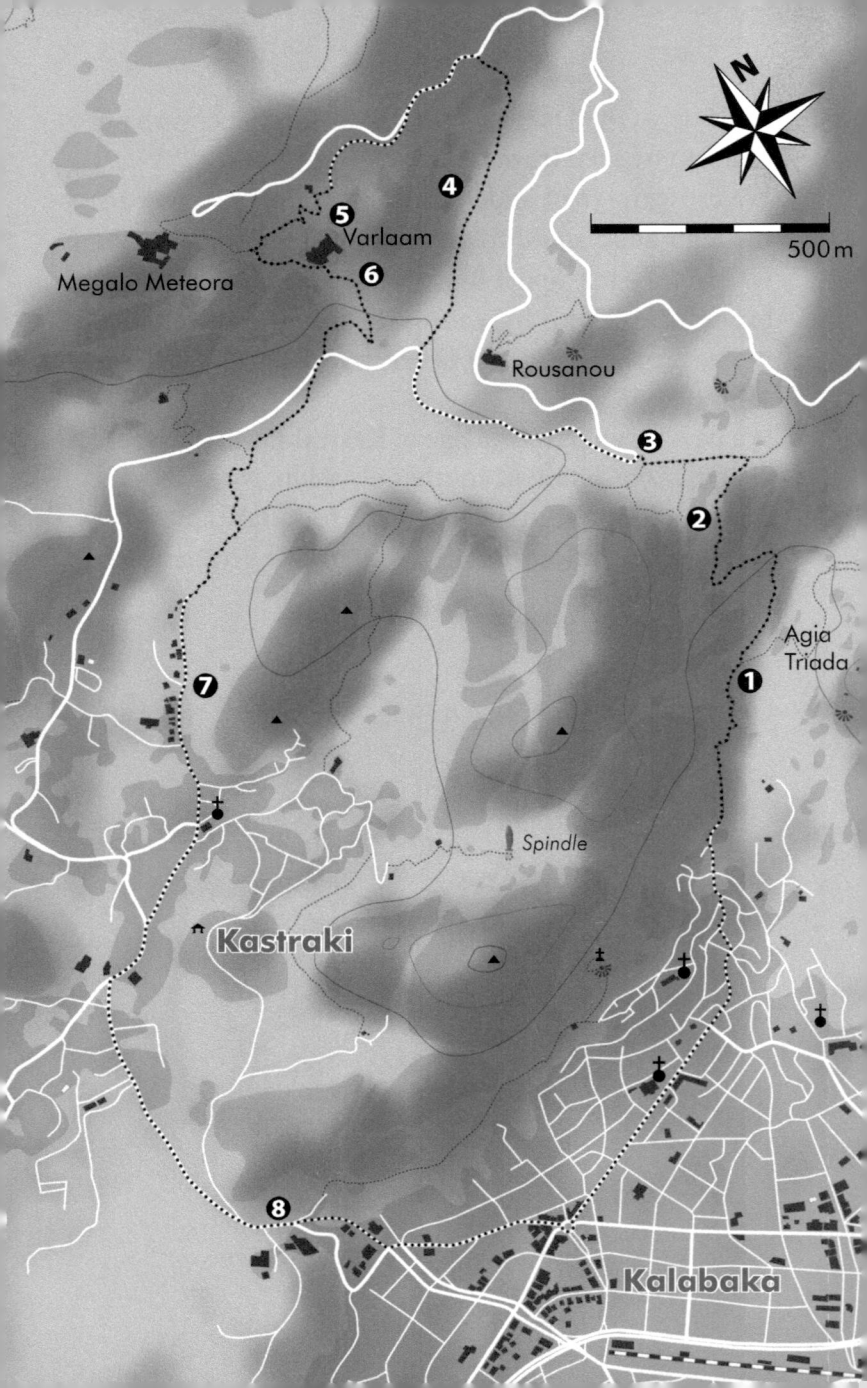

N

500 m

4

5 Varlaam

6

Megalo Meteora

Rousanou

3

2

Agia
Triada

1

7

Spindle

Kastraki

8

Kalabaka

3. Hiking route: Through upper Kastraki via the Monk's Prison to the Doupiani Church (Agios Nikolaos)

This route takes us to old monasteries hewn out of the rock, a prison for monks and probably the oldest little church in the Meteor region. We also cross a mountain cleft and visit the spindle. There is an opportunity to visit a monastery. For the very brave without fear of heights, the climb up the Holy Spirit Massif is the highlight. The hiking route is relatively long, in some places you need stamina, good footwear is necessary. Without ascent to the Holy Spirit about 3 to 3 ½ hours.

We start our hike in the centre of Kalabaka and walk towards Kastraki. At the upper end of the village, shortly after the restaurant 'Panorama', we turn right towards Kastraki, more precisely to the upper part of the village. After the first bend to the right, we reach a rocky valley where the monks of earlier centuries carried out a variety of activities ❶. This place must have been teeming with them...

Immediately to the right, before the entrance to the gorge, we see former hermit caves, which were later used by shepherds as shelters and pantries. There are often water containers in front of them for the roaming herd of goats. A few metres further on, a steep road goes up on the right and into the valley.

Many Greeks always want to drive directly to their destination. We should therefore not be surprised if they also drive right up to the door of this ensemble of chapel and monastery.

On the right wall we see the Nikolaos Bandova Monastery carved into the rock, which cannot be visited. However, we can walk up the stone steps on the slope and enjoy a beautiful view of Kalabaka. Back down again, just ahead of us is the small chapel of Panagia Phaneromeni, behind it the monastery of Agia Trias, Asketirion of the monastery of Agios Nikolaos.

Carved into the rock we see other former monasteries Agios Antonios and Agios Gregorios, whose wooden balconies are clearly visible.

If you turn very close to the rock to the left, you can take a small path through scrub and over the bare stone to above Kastraki, thus shortening the way to the spindle. We return to the road and walk uphill to the right to a shelter ❷ that offers protection from both rain and sun and a beautiful view of the valley of the Pinios: to the left rises the peak of the Koziakas massif with the summer village of Koromilia, and in front of it, nestled at the foot of the mountain, the village of Diava. Halfway down on the right is the village of Kastraki, behind which we can make out the river Pinios. On the far right, we can see the neat little church of Doupiani in front of the rock of the same name and the northern Meteora massif, on which the

Monastery of Nikolaos Bantova
Spindle seen from Kast
Ascent to the Holy Spirit Rock

main monastery of Metamorfosis and Varlaam are located. The monastery of Rousanou can be seen on the far right through a gap between two rocks.

After a short rest we continue our way and reach the first houses of the upper part of Kastraki. They are simple little houses in narrow alleys, some are already dilapidated. Further down towards the centre, however, several historic mansions have been renovated in the old style. They are rented out or serve as hotels or taverns. At least you get a good impression of what this mountain village might have looked like in the past.

We turn right and walk uphill to the church of Agios Nikolaos. There a stairway begins that leads us to another little church, Panagia Koimesis Theotokou ❷. From here we climb a beaten path to the Spindle ❸, a towering rock nose so called because of its peculiar shape. It is often used as a training ground for novice climbers. It is prominently visible from several points in Kastraki, including the central church forecourt.

We go back along the path until we reach the first houses and keep to the right until we see a sign with a salamander. We follow the path downhill and turn right at the fork ❹, turning left into the village. Now we cross a small valley with abandoned buildings, climb up again and walk across meadows to the foot of the Holy Spirit Rock. We follow the marked path

Agios Nikolaos Anapavsas
Panagia Doupiani

until we reach a fork. To the left we go up to the Holy Spirit Rock, the path is partly secured with a railing and only something for people without a fear of heights, because it is very steep. On the plateau you can see the ruins of old monastery buildings. The view of Kastraki and beyond is overwhelming.

The safer path continues up to the saddle on the right, from where we now have a view of the northern meteoric monasteries of Metamorfosis, Varlaam and Rousanou. As we descend, we keep very close to the rock and practically turn left around it. We are right in front of the old monk's prison ❺, to whose cavity we climb up. We can well imagine why a monk had to 'serve time' here: theft, idolatry, image worship, carnal lust, heresy...

Monks were and are only human!

We now descend the Paleocranie valley until we come out at a pump house ❻. Just before it, we can admire ancient trees. At the little house we can go left to Kastraki if we are tired. Going up on the right, after ten minutes we come to the monastery of Agios Nikolaos ❼.

On the way back on the road, at the entrance to Kastraki, we visit the small church at Doupiani Rock ❽, one of the first buildings erected by monks in the Meteora area.

Coming from the little church, we cross the main road, cross a small valley and turn right at the primary school. In a few minutes we are at the church square in Kastraki **❾** and from there we come to Kalabaka on familiar paths (see route 2,3).

4. Hiking route: About the Lying Tomcat around the Meteora rocks (Agios Ipapantis, Agios Varlaam, Agios Metamorfosis)

On this hike we walk around the meteor rocks, all paths are safe even for non-climbers. On the way we have the opportunity to visit the oldest little church in the region and a monastery hidden in the rock. Return by bus at the Metamorfosis monastery. Duration about 2 ½ hrs.

We start our hike in the centre of Kalabaka and walk to the neighbouring village of Kastraki. This time we follow the main road until the road goes up to the village square of Kastraki on the right at a small bakery. We cross the village and turn left at the school, down the valley and immediately up again. We cross the main road and see the small Doupiani church ❶ above us on the right, the oldest remnant from the beginnings of monk settlement in the Middle Ages (1160). This is where the monks are said to have gathered regularly, and from here they gradually developed the entire area. We go down again on the small road, turn right and reach the neighbouring rock, the Lying Tomcat ❷. It stretches gently from south to north and is very easy to climb. From the top we have a magnificent view of Kastraki and the northern and southern

Lying Tomcat
Monastery of Ipapantis
Paleocrania Valley

meteoric rocks. The descent on the north side next to the Doupiani Rock is a little steeper, but not at all dangerous. We reach a dirt road, which we follow to the left. We cross the asphalt road and walk slightly uphill towards the prominent turrets of the western meteoric rocks. On the left, above the path, we can see old caves that today occasionally serve as shelters for cattle and shepherds. Immediately in front of the two neighbouring towers on the left ❸, a groove opens up through which we can easily reach the other side of the rocks. Here, the view is instantly different and the atmosphere changes. We look at sheep farms, hear their bells in the distance, but of course also the sounds of engines of various farming activities. We walk along a fairly wide footpath on the slope of the cliffs, below us runs the asphalt road to the farmsteads. To the left of the path, large meadows appear again and again, after a while a drinking trough. Sometimes a herd of cows runs in front of us, very good-natured, a little timid animals. Twice we descend deeply into the valley of a stream, which has water until about mid-April and from the end of October.

It is always pleasantly cool here in the hot sun. When it rains in spring or autumn, fire salamanders sit on the path every 20 metres, making their way away very sluggishly and clumsily. Down by the road, you may encounter a pack of ten to fifteen medium-sized dogs, snarling in attack. You should always have a stick with you, the animals immediately retreat in fear.

From the forest path we come to a sandy road, which we follow upwards to the right, around the steep rock into which the hidden monastery of Ipapantis ❹ was carved. It now has a lift and the interior is comfortable. Unfortunately, it is not open to visitors at the moment.

We walk uphill past the picturesque monastery and at the bottom of the climb we first turn left. We reach a plateau where the monument to the freedom fighter of Vlachava ❺ attracts our attention. It commemorates the struggles of the Greek freedom fighters against the Ottoman foreign rulers. We go back to the turnoff and now follow the path that makes us gain height quickly. On the way, we see one or the other hollow where wild boars regularly wallow. A few kilometres away from the meteor rocks, they are occasionally seen in broad daylight, but understandably only at night in the tourist area.

After a few metres we reach a small plateau and now circle a funnel-shaped deep valley. Every few metres we have a new perspective on the rock formations staggered in the depths. There is complete silence here, although we are only 15 minutes away from the main artery, the access road ❻ to the two important monasteries of Varlaam and Metamorfosis. On some days, up to a hundred buses and countless cars roar up it. Whole groups of tourists move up the stairs at a snail's pace, talking loudly.

At the end of the cauldron, it is only a few steps uphill and we can clearly hear the sound of engines, look down at the road and the Varlaam monastery. Our hike ends here, the return journey is by bus from the Metamorfosis monastery ❼, a few metres uphill.

Monastery Agios Metamorfosis (Megalo Meteoro)

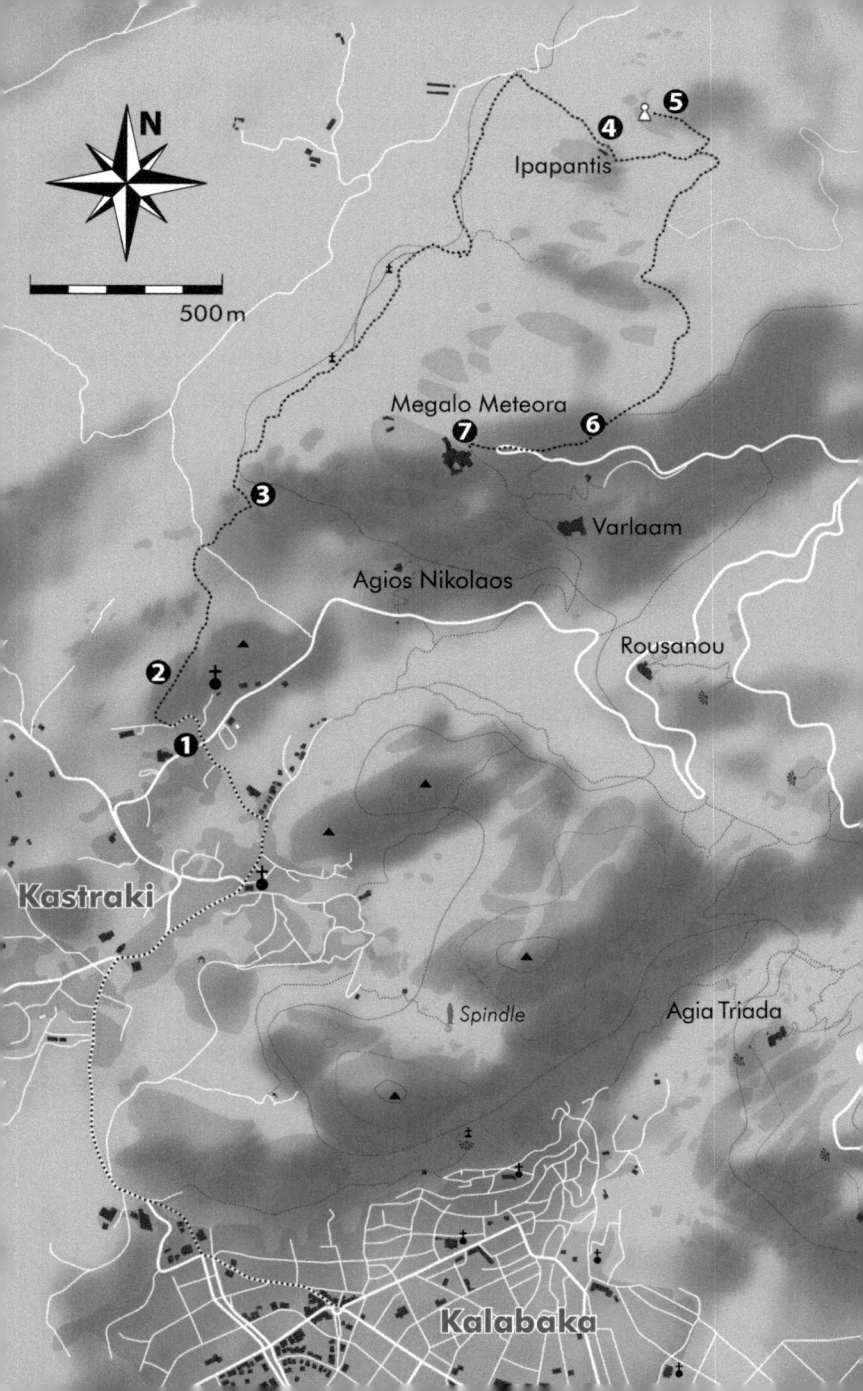

5. Hiking route: From the great monasteries to the mountainous countryside (Agios Varlaam, Agios Metamorfosis, Agia Triada)

On this hiking tour we move relatively far away from the Meteora monasteries and gain completely new views of them. There is an opportunity to visit three monasteries on the way. The pure hiking time is about 3 to 3 ½ hours.

We take the bus to the monastery of Metamorfosis ❶. There we climb the opposite rock, in several places there are regular steps. We walk on a narrow path towards the east, leaving the Varlaam monastery below us. At the fork ❷ we take the right path, on the left we descend to the hidden rock monastery of Ipapantis (see route 4). Here we enjoy a beautiful view of the distant Pindos Mountains, on the right we look down on the serpentines of the monastery feeder road. Now we climb a hill and reach a small meadow and finally a large plateau ❸ between the monasteries and the village of Vlachava. You can make out the place in the distance. From the highest point of the meadow you can see Mount Olympus on a clear day.

Ornithologists have the opportunity to observe a rare species of vulture, the Egyptian vulture (Neophron percnopterus) (see also illustration on page 6).

Monastery of Agios Metamorfosis
Far view to the northeast
Agia Triada Monastery in front of Koziakas Mountain

However, only one pair of the once hunted and now protected bird species was sighted in 2018.

A dirt road runs along the meadow, which we follow at first. The Meteora Track Race (MTR), a cross-country race of the highest difficulty that leads through the bizarre mountains around Kalabaka, takes place on this terrain every year. It is attended by runners from many countries and takes place on Ochi Day (28 October).

Leave the path at a small church with an image of a saint (Proskinitario) and go downhill on the meadow to the right. Passing a cattle trough ❹, we feel our way along a narrow rivulet, which requires a little orientation. If we leave the rivulet, which is dry for the longest time of the year, to the left below us, we should not miss the path. After a few minutes we reach a mountain meadow, which we cross. It goes without saying that we should in no way be afraid of the cows, which we can encounter at any time on this section of our hike.

From the meadow we enter a deciduous forest again and after another ten minutes we come out at the road from Kalabaka to Vlachava ❺, above the turnoff to the monasteries of Agia Triada and Agios Stefanos. We now have the option of going left uphill along the road to reach the Tzertzi excursion area after a few hundred metres, an extensive area with seating, wooden tables, a paved dance floor (!) and a small church. Here the locals celebrate May Day with food, drink

and song. Another nice resting place presents itself as we walk a hundred metres downhill from where we came out. Above a cattle trough, which lies directly on the asphalt road, a meadow invites us to have a picnic. Now we make our way home. To do so, we cross the road and use the old path to the left below it. We go past old trees, through bushes, sometimes on a narrow ridge along the slope (you can walk this part on the road next door if you do not have the necessary sure-footedness!) Finally we reach a large stony meadow, at the end of which the hairpin bend ❻ of the road from Kalabaka to Vlachava as well as the turnoff to the monasteries of Varlaam and Metamorfosis can be seen.

We stay in the upper part of the meadow and easily find the path that goes along above the road. It takes us to the junction directly opposite the mountain of St. Stephen ❼.

Here we can now choose whether to go around St. Stephen's mountain to Kalabaka (see route 1) or take the descent at Agia Triada Monastery (like route 1 in the opposite direction)!

6. Hiking route: Via the dragon's cave to the great monasteries (Agios Nikolaos, Agios Varlaam, Agios Metamorfosis)

On this route we have the opportunity to visit several monasteries. The way back can either be done by bus or on one of the already described sections. The outward journey takes 1 to 1 ½ hours, with the return journey about 3 hours.

We walk from Kalabaka to Kastraki, just as we like, through the upper part of the village or along the main road, to the main church of Peter and Paul ❶ in the church square. To the west and south of the square we find several taverns for small and large appetites or a drink. To the north is the Geological Museum for the inquisitive. We walk past the main square and spot colourful scarves hanging high up on the right from a rock niche of the Holy Spirit Rock. Every year on 23 April, young people from the village climb up from the church of St George the Dragonslayer to the rock where the remains of the old monastery of St George Mandilas ❷ are located. The whole village gathers to perform the liturgy with the priest and then eat cakes, coffee and wine at long tables. As far as fixed church holidays are concerned, the Greek Orthodox Church follows the Gregorian calendar, celebrating Christmas on 25 December and Saint George's Day on 23 April.

The other Orthodox Churches, on the other hand, e.g. also the Russian and Serbian, celebrate Christmas on 7 January and Saint George on 6 May.

We continue our way in a northerly direction out of the village, directly towards the meteor rocks. On the left, the path descends relatively steeply, a watercourse collects the mountain rivulets and leads them to Pinios. The path makes a few bends through a small valley and climbs again. At this point there is a junction where we reach the monastery of Agios Nikolaos Anapavsas ❸ in five minutes on the left.

Shortly afterwards, we reach the asphalt road on the right, which we cross. Unfortunately, the beautiful bench at this point has not been replaced after board after board became rotten and fell off. Therefore, we hike straight on uphill. After only a few metres, we cross a non-existent obstacle on a reconstructed stone bridge. It seems a little out of place and artificial. Halfway up, we see the dragon's cave ❹ above us on the right, to which a small path leads. We can climb up and admire the spacious cave. Its jagged outline can be seen from afar, both from the asphalt road and from the hiking trails opposite.

After inspecting the cave, we continue to climb. On 'bad' days we soon hear a 'hellish noise', i.e. quite a lot and loud tourist voices. This is not for meditative, religious pilgrims! But we know that in advance, that

Monastery of Agios Georgios Mantilas
Varlaam Monastery, Dragon's Cave (bottom)

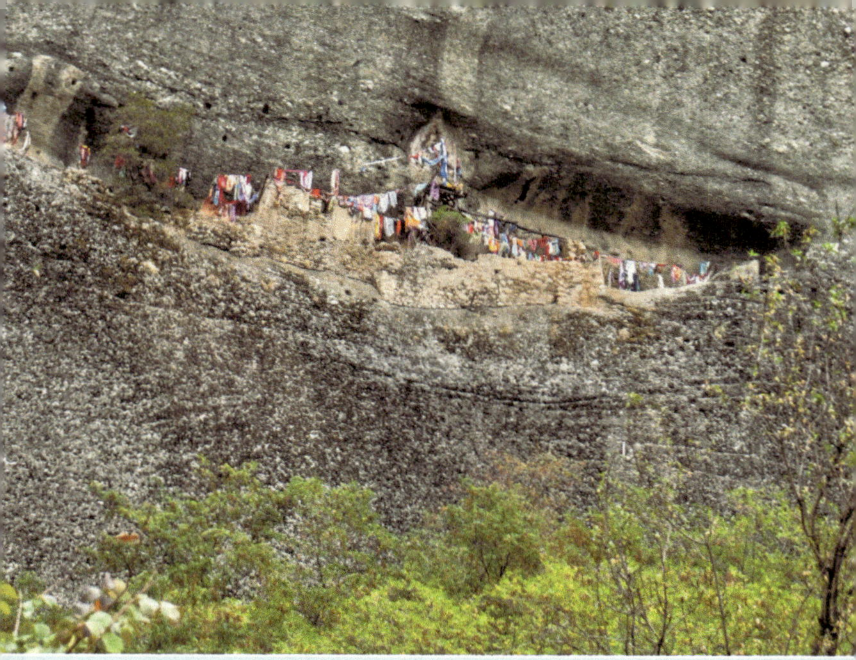

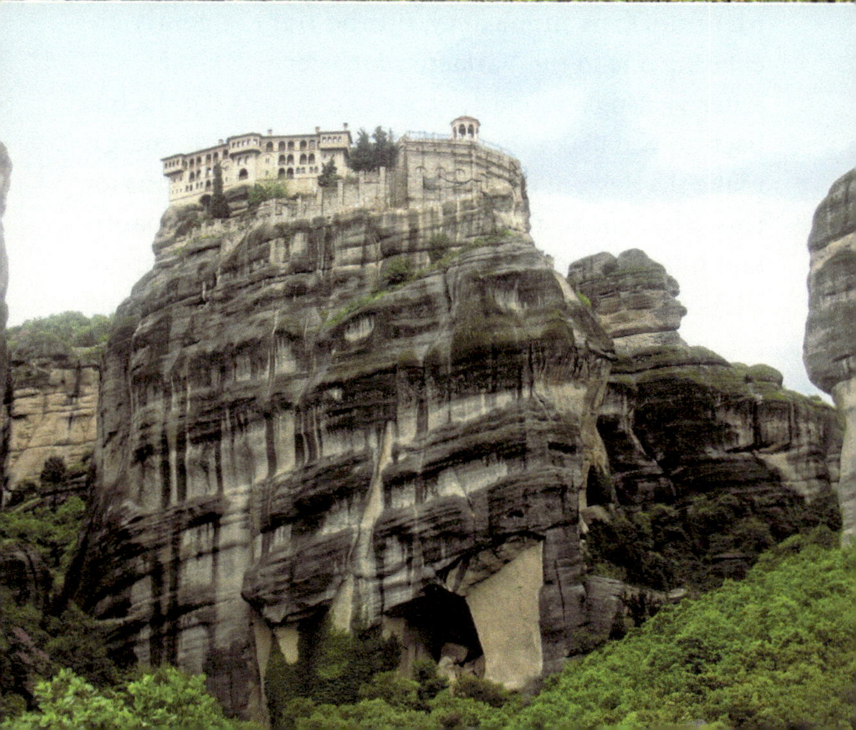

we have to share these magical, inspirational sites - with about 2 to 3 million people a year and of course they all have to pass through the main monasteries once. It goes without saying that not all of them have undergone a basic course in religious decorum, so it is sometimes necessary to ask for silence when, on the most important holiday of the whole year, Easter, during (!) the holy liturgy right in front of the entrance to the most famous church in the place, a troop of Dutch tourists made such a big noise that it was overheard in the church. Fortunately, almost no one understood the content of the conversation!

At the fork in the path ❺, we now have to decide: on the left, a somewhat steeper path leads to the Metamorfosis monastery, on the right, a gently ascending one to the Varlaam monastery.

After visiting a monastery, we can either take the bus back to Kalabaka or, if we still have enough energy, make the descent on foot. There are longer options for this: Descent to the hidden monastery of Ipapantis and hike around the rocks to Kastraki (route 4 opposite) or shorter ones: Descent via the Cat Church and ascent at the Rousanou hairpin bend (Route 2 opposite).

N

500 m

Megalo Meteora

⑤

Varlaam

Agios Nikolaos

④

③

Rousanou

②

①

Kastraki

Spindle

Kalabaka

7. Hiking route: Via the shepherd's hut to the monastery of Agios Rousanou (Agia Triada, Agia Rousanou)

On this route we also pass several monasteries. We also walk through dense bushes and see ancient trees in the valley of a small river.

Duration 2 ½ hours.

We take the footpath to the monastery of Agia Triada on the north-western edge of Kalabaka, above the Byzantine church (see route 1). After two thirds of the way there is a large rock in the middle of the path ❶ there we turn left into a small hollow way.

Note: If you want to visit the monastery of Agia Triada, climb a little further and then return to the starting point. The path is a little uneven, in two or three places it requires a certain amount of surefootedness. But it is not dangerous if you wear sensible footwear. We walk slightly uphill below the asphalt road to the monastery of Agios Stefanos, come very close to the road and then go downhill to a mountain meadow. Occasionally we meet a herd of goats or a cow. Thus, this locality no longer lives up to its traditional name of 'shepherd's hut'; the time of flocks of sheep in this place is over!

Rousanou Monastery
Monastery garden
View with the monasteries Agios Nikolaos, Rousanou, Metamorfosis

At the bottom of the meadow ❷, by the little stream, we turn up to the left and now walk on a narrow path below the asphalt road to the monastery of Metamorfosis. It always offers beautiful views, especially at its highest point: to the south we see the monastery of Agia Triada and behind it, far below, Kalabaka; to the west we see the rock formations of the middle massif lined up one after the other, on which no monasteries are preserved; to the north our view falls on the monasteries of Rousanou and Varlaam; finally, to the east we see the hill of St Stephen and behind it the wide hinterland towards Trikala.

We keep to the right at this highest point and reach the asphalt road, which we follow turning left. After a few metres, we reach an 'official' viewpoint ❸, where it is not uncommon for there to be a lot of crowds (and shouting); admittedly, the view here is even more spectacular than the one just described, but less meditative to enjoy.

We now continue along the road for a few hundred metres and arrive at another viewpoint ❹ with spectacular views. The same applies as for the previous one. Immediately behind it, a stairway path descends to the Rousanou nunnery. For once, we join the stream of tourists and walk downhill to the monastery buildings we can visit ❺.

At the bottom of the road, turn left and continue downhill. At the hairpin bend ❻ there is a small place that hikers or climbers like to use as a car park.

Unlike us, they drive 'right up to the front door', so to speak, and only hike a small part of our tours. At the edge of this place, a path goes down into a hollow.

There is a fork: one goes directly uphill and leads over the ridge to Kalabaka (see Route 2 opposite), we take the other, which first runs parallel to the road in the ditch and then leads gently uphill. We are now moving above the Paleokranies valley. To the left, the rocks of the Holy Spirit Massif with the Monk's Prison look out at us, to the right we see the Dragon's Cave on the opposite side, above it the Varlaam Monastery, and on the far right Rousanou, where we have just come from. We finally descend into the valley, passing ancient trees. At the pump house ❼ we come to the path to Kastraki, which we already know from other tours (routes 2, 3).

Through Kastraki we go back to Kalabaka.

8. Hiking route: In the Triskianos Valley

On this route we leave the area of the Meteora rocks and hike into the neighbouring valley, where we cover a circular route over mountain ridges, hollow paths, past bizarre rock formations. Several times we are offered magnificent panoramic views.

Duration of the hike 5 to 5 ½ hours.

We start in the centre of Kalabaka and walk to the neighbouring village of Kastraki. At the turnoff to the centre, we stay on the main road, then take the next road to the left of it, at the Hotel Meteoritis (perhaps named after a new kind of tourist disease?).

We follow this road through the western part and catch a glimpseof the five-star hotel 'Meteora' from afar, not to be confused with the family-run hotel of the same name in Kalabaka! We pass the cemetery, cross a small pass and go down into the village part of Kastraki ❶. The asphalt road we walk on is hardly frequented. There is currently a large construction site on the busy E 92 from Larissa to Ioannina, which we walk along until we reach a taverna with a large car park in front. There we turn right into the path (sign-post Agia Paraskevi) ❷.

The initially gentle chains of hills slowly pile up to a high massif on the right (Oat Sack Rocks, Dragon rocks).

Our path leads us along a dried up, stony riverbed covered with large, old oaks.

In winter and after the snow melts, a raging mountain stream can form; it carries water until March.

Through extensive meadows and pastures we come deeper into the Triskiano valley, which is now lined with larger photovoltaic plants. Sometimes we see a flock of sheep far away, medium-sized dogs stalk us from a proper distance. They are mostly good natured, but it is advisable to carry a stick with you on all hikes.

At a fork in the road, we keep to the right and after 15 minutes we pass through a small wood onto a large meadow. The little church of Agia Paraskevi ❸ is a remnant of the old settlement of Paliohori, of which nothing else can be seen. We cross the meadow and walk uphill on the upper left edge along a forest path and after about 500 metres we reach the sheep rocks ❹, a loose formation of individual blocks or peaks. We head east on a narrow path and now turn south slightly along the slope. Finally, we reach the Dragon Rocks ❺, from where we can enjoy a beautiful view. We continue our way in a south-westerly direction on a narrow ridge and reach the Oat Sack Rocks ❻, which once again grant us a wide view of the surrounding countryside.

The descent is via a path on the left that soon bends to the right and becomes a forest path. We follow it

Oat Sack Rocks
Sheep Rocks, Dragon Rocks in the Triskianos Valley
On the Oat Sack Rocks

downhill for about 20 minutes until we spot a stream depression low down. We descend carefully, it is relatively steep, cross the depression and at the other end climb up into a huge pasture area ❼.

We keep to the right of the valley of the stream (mostly dry) and return to the village part of Kastraki. At the crossroads by the first homestead ❽, go straight ahead through a wide stream (at high water, turn left over the wooden bridge).

Passing a small homestead, we walk up towards the meteor rocks, which we can already see from afar. Every now and then we see a sign 'No hunting' (Απαγορέυεται το κυνήγι), which, according to experience, indicates that there is at least occasional hunting. (There are also quite a few used cartridges to be found by the wayside!)

At the top of the asphalt road ❾, we keep to the right, circle the northwestern meteor rocks and can now decide how to end our hike today. Either via the Lying Tomcat (then turn right before the Doupiani Rock, see route 4 opposite) or straight on to the main road and then right through Kastraki to Kalabaka.

From time to time you meet it here along the path,
the salinos's thessalian rat - rattus thessalus

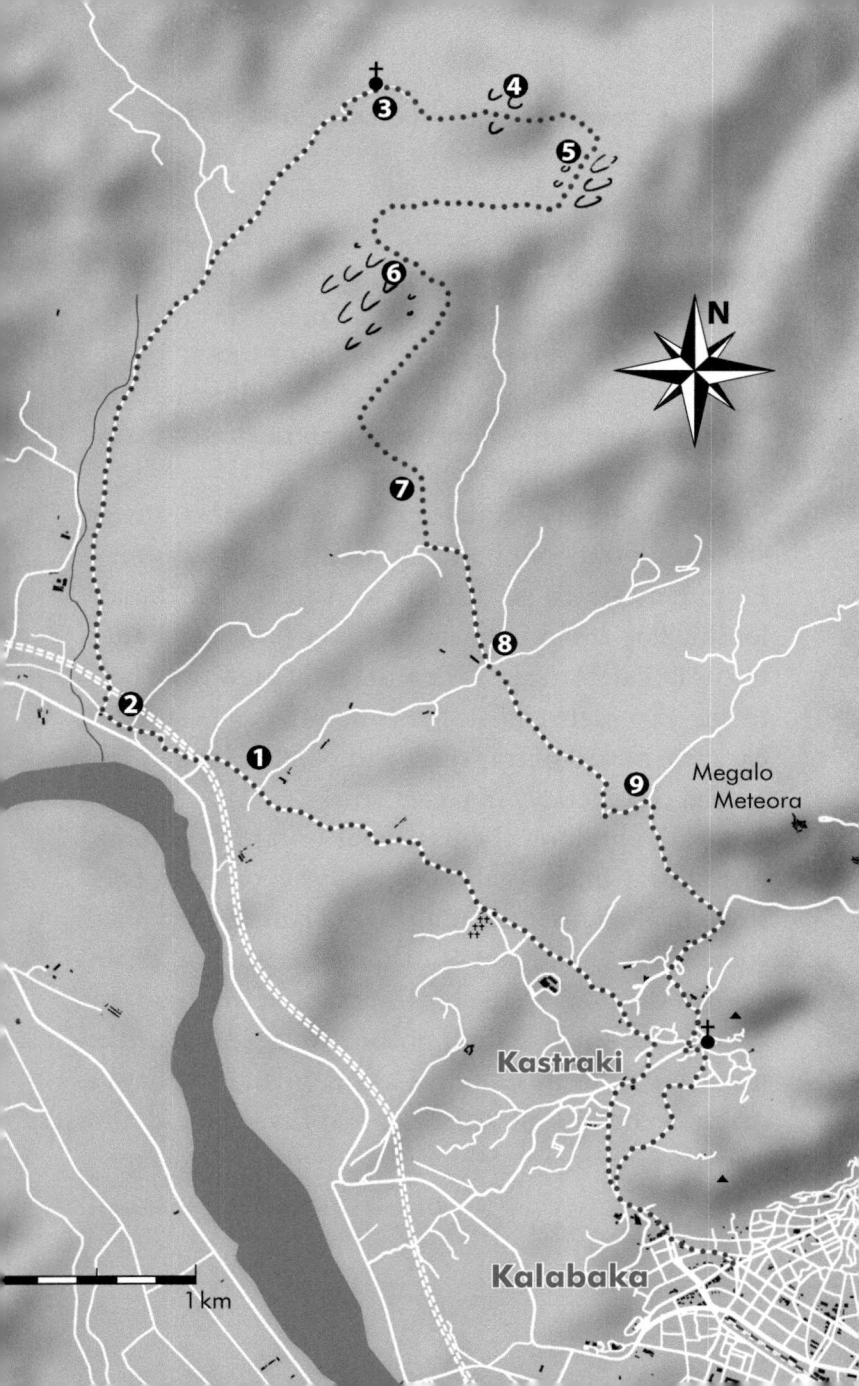

N

③

④

⑤

⑥

⑦

⑧

⑨ Megalo
Meteora

②

①

Kastraki

Kalabaka

1 km

9. Hiking route: The neighbouring villages Diava and Sarakina

We visit the neighbouring villages of Diava and Sarakina on the other side of the river Pinios. On the way we can find the remains of a Roman fort (Kastro) as well as an old bridge from Byzantine times.

A spring river under dense trees provides reliable shade even in high summer. The walking time - mainly on asphalt - is about 3 ½ hours.

From the centre of Kalabaka we walk to the railway station, a pretty old building from the 19th century. From here trains go directly to Athens and Thessaloniki. For some connections you have to change trains in Paleofarsalos. There are only a few from here to the two metropolises, but the railway is still the cheapest means of transport and punctuality has improved considerably in recent years.

We walk uphill on the pavement towards Ioannina. The railway line was also originally supposed to continue in this direction. But these plans got stranded somewhere in the abyss of Greek economic problems in the past. At the highest point of this road, we can see the small church of the Prophet Ilias on the house hill ❶ above us on the left. From here we have a magnificent view of Kalabaka and the southern and

Brook spring near Diava
General view Kalabaka and Meteora
Bridge in Sarakina

eastern Meteoric Rocks, to the west we look towards Pinios and the distant Pindos Mountains, to the south towards the Koziakas Mountains with the offshore villages of Diava and Sarakina, which we want to visit. Just below the summit we make out the summer houses of Koromilia.

We walk a few metres along the main road, past the hospital, in front of which a kiosk and fruit and vegetable sellers offer their wares, and then turn left towards the stadium. The Greek football season starts in autumn and ends early in the year because of the great heat from May to September.

At the stadium we turn right and pass the sports hall. Unfortunately, we now have to walk along a moderately busy road until Diava. Now and then there are wider verges, so that walking is bearable. After only a few hundred metres we come to the bridge over the Pinios ❷. It is one of the longest rivers in Greece with 217 km and dominates the Thessalian lowlands. The headwaters are in southern Pindos, the mouth into the Aegean Sea north of Larissa, not far from Mount Olympus. Here, just before Diava, this river looks completely inconspicuous most of the year, especially during the main tourist season from April to October. It hardly carries any water in summer, so there is no question of 'flowing'. You can wade through it to get to the other side. But make no mistake: at snowmelt time, the Pinios can swell enormously and become a monster.

A few years ago (2016), the stream completely destroyed the bridge in spring! The inhabitants of Diava had to take long detours to get to Kalabaka. In summer, most drove their cars, tractors or trucks through shallow fords to save time. Today, the new bridge has been completed.

The river and its immediate surroundings are not exactly inviting. It is true that there is only a few places where rubbish lies around; this bad habit of the locals is gradually being curbed. But firstly, there are no real paths, and secondly, there is nothing special to see, apart from a few water birds.

Instead, you have to reckon with stray dogs.

On the northern side of the Pinio, the village of Diava begins, namely the industrial and craft part: petrol station, lime works, sawmill, car mechanic (here you can admire ancient tractor types rusting away). At the crossroads we can decide whether we want to go into the village or stay in nature. In Diava, a completely new church has been built on the meadow, of course in classical Orthodox style.

For an Orthodox Christian, it is almost unthinkable what Western Christians apparently long for, to build so-called modern church buildings. Admittedly, in Germany, for example, some of these abstract buildings from the 60s/70s of the last century have already been desecrated and used for other purposes.

You haven't heard anything like that from Orthodox churches yet!

Leaving the village on the right, we take the narrow asphalt road towards Sarakina. After a few hundred metres, we turn right onto a sandy path. The signpost is renewed every now and then, it promises more sights (excursion restaurant, mountain bike route, Kastro, spring and some more!) than it can deliver, as we will see. Anyway, after 15 minutes we reach the first destination, a beautiful spring grove ❸ with large, shady trees and a lively babbling brook. Many locals come here with their cars to fill more or less numerous containers with the water. If the Greek in the rural area has the opportunity to take his drinking water from a spring, he always prefers it to tap water.

Now we go up the path past the spring. The higher we get, the more beautiful the view of the Meteor rocks and the lonely rock of Theopetra five kilometres to the east becomes. If we are lucky, we discover a sign 'καστρο' in a bush on the left or even find the narrow path on the right that leads us to the site of an ancient fortress ❹ at a strategically important position. Unfortunately, it was used as a natural quarry for a long time, and older structures are no longer recognisable to the layman.

At least one can imagine a tower on the top of the rock and recognise the strategic value, because one can control the entire river plain far beyond Trikala.

Snowy Koziakas Mountains in Spring
Greek tortoise
Theopetra Rock

We leave this dreary place and walk to the asphalt road that leads from Agia Paraskevi to Sarakina. There we turn left and at the crossroads we reach the small church of Agios Athanasios ❺ built on the rock. It invites you to take a nice rest.

We now leave the car road and keep to the left. From far away we can see the old bridge ❻ from the 15th century over the Pinios. It has withstood all catastrophes and wars, but unfortunately it is not maintained. Of course, it is closed to cars, but long after the Second World War farmers were still crossing it with horse-drawn carts or tractors. Due to its boldly curved arch, it was never in danger of being destroyed by floods, unlike the newfangled one in Diava.

Once we have crossed the bridge, we are at the edge of the village of Sarakina. Right at the entrance to the village, on the left directly on the huge rock, is the small picturesque church Agion Apostolon ❼, in front of it the cemetery. The village of Sarakina offers no other sights, so we make our way back. Unfortunately, this part of the hike is less attractive, although quite instructive. We leave it to intuition or free choice, the rough direction is clear, one can walk 'on sight'.

There is a choice of an asphalt road directly to Kalabaka, parallel field paths, straying along the river (practically no paths) and in sections on the filled-in route of a bypass road that has not (yet) been built. Here one can say with a clear conscience:

'All roads lead to Kalabaka!'

10. City walk: The village of Kalabaka

On this route we get to know the village of Kalabaka and its immediate surroundings in more detail.

We will present a circular route and some prominent points in the centre. The circular route can be interrupted or ended at any time or continued at another point.

First, something about the name Kalabaka. There are two ways of writing it: Kalabaka and Kalampaka, which leads quite a few people to pronounce the 'p' clearly. That is wrong! The name is always pronounced softly 'b' in Greek. This misunderstanding arose from the Greek spelling 'Καλαμπακα', literally 'Kalampaka'. Now, there are no letters for 'b, d, g' in the Greek script, these sounds did not originally occur in this language, rather the clearly distinguished 'β, δ, γ'. So when a 'b, d, g' was imported from foreign languages, something had to be devised. One agreed on: μπ for 'b', ντ for 'd' and γκ for 'g'. That is why beer is written μπιρα but pronounced 'bira'. So it follows that the present name for the town is not Greek, but comes from Turkish, it comes from 'kalempak', 'neat fortress'. We start at the 'Town Hall Square' ❶, which takes its name from the 'Δημαρχος', the mayor. Here is also a stop of the Meteorabus line, which runs three times a day

Busts on Rigas Feraios Square
Kalabaka before sunrise
Byzantine Church 'Koimesis tis Theotokou'

to and from the monasteries during the season. All the shops important for tourists can be found around the square: café, restaurant, kiosk, bakery, souvenir shops, tourist information, grocers, confectioners, hotels. In a side street there is a library in a nice building. The bus station is a 5-minute walk away.

We now stroll down Trikalon Street, the main axis of Kalabaka. As the name suggests, it comes from the district capital of Trikkala, runs dead straight through the town to lead out of the town towards Ioannina at the town hall square as Ioanninon Street. However, through traffic is routed on the outskirts of the centre via Pindou Street past the railway station and joins the main road at the western end of Kalabaka.

Grammatical digression on the street names: the reference words of the names are in the genitive, the 2nd case, because they are in the construction 'street of/ of...'. Trikalon Street is thus the 'street of the city of Trikkala', in Greek 'οδος των Τρικκαλων', in short 'Trikalon'. Thus, the 'road of Pindos' becomes the Pindou road through the Greek genitive 'Pindou'.

In the upper part of Trikalon Street, normal shops predominate, there are only a few shops of a tourist nature. However, we unfortunately have to realise that more and more shops have to close down every year. This is partly due to the long-term consequences of the devastating economic crisis that began in 2012.

But it is probably also due to the changing composition of tourists. Most of them pass by the place in daily busloads, being fed in big restaurants on the outskirts of Kalabaka after visiting the monasteries, before quickly moving on. It is hard to imagine what will remain after the Corona years or what will be built on a completely new basis.

Continuing along Trikalon Street, we come to Rigas Fereos Square ❷, named after the writer and revolutionary Rigas Velestinlis, a native of Pherai. Young and old meet here every evening to chat and stroll. On public holidays, there are rallies and marches. The busts of two regional freedom fighters are erected in the square.

In the side street Chatzipetrou is the small but very interesting 'Greek Education Museum' ❸. It houses a large collection of school and textbooks, translations of the Greek classics into other world languages and a re-enactment of a 19th century Greek classroom.

As we continue our walk, we now enter the 'touristy' eastern part of Trikalon Street. Cafés and snack restaurants crowd Dimoula Square, which seems a little listless. This is where the youth meets for a drink. At the end of the narrower centre, to the left and right are large hotel complexes supplied by daily bus loads. The people who stay here rarely stay longer than one night. Their calculation goes like this:

Arrival day = 2 to 3 monasteries, stay overnight, another 2 to 3 monasteries, departure.

Between Trikalon Street and the Pindou thorough-fare is the Natural History Museum with dioramas and information about animal species, the ecosystem and a mushroom collection ❹. It is definitely worth a visit, for example on a rainy day.

We turn left off Trikalon Street into Zacharia Psyra uphill to reach the large, newly built church Meteoron Pateron ❺. It is a beautiful sacred building, a feast for the eyes, even if it does not have a long tradition. On the other hand, its name radiates dignity and tradition: Church of the Holy Fathers of Meteora (Ιερός Ναός Οσίων Μετεωριτών Πατέρων).

We follow the road uphill until we reach Analipseos Street, where we turn left. It leads us to the military cemetery with the little church of Agios Demetrios ❻. Here lie buried victims of the Greek Civil War, which began immediately with the end of the Second World War and lasted until 1949. The cemetery is only open on Ochi Day (28.10.).

From here, we tend to keep to the right and wander through small narrow streets ❼ in one of the oldest parts of the city. On the city map, the difference in the street layout is easy to distinguish. The northern part of the city up to the south of Vlachava Street and then D. Liapidi and Geka Streets consists of an irregular network of streets and alleys that are laid out uphill.

Ochi Day Parade
Tavern in Kalabaka
Town hall

The parts of the city to the south are more or less geometrically laid out, rectangular or rhombic. The older part corresponds to the Ottoman type, the southern newer one was subject to European urban planning criteria.

We now turn to the jewel among the churches, the Byzantine Church of the Assumption of the Virgin Mary (Ναός της Κοιμήσεως της Θεοτόκου) ❸ from the 12th century. A visit to the interior is definitely recommended because of the wall paintings. Although the building is heavily repaired in many places, it contains some interesting spolia, especially on the south façade. Behind the church is the chapel of Agios Pantos in the old cemetery. In the Byzantine church, the holy liturgy is traditionally celebrated on Easter Monday. Above the church runs a narrow road, which we follow to the left. We are now walking along the uppermost edge of the town, so to speak. We come across another little church and ruins of old houses. This is the oldest part of the town from a time when there was no tourism. At that time, many pilgrims came to the region to stay in the monasteries.

If we continue directly along the rock on a path, we come out at a picnic area above the 'Panorama' restaurant ❾. We can also go downhill beforehand and then reach the shortcut road below this restaurant. From there, it is only a stone's throw to the 'Digital Projection Center of Meteora's History & Culture' ❿, in the building of the former Folklore Museum (since

2017). Here you can get a vivid impression of the history and culture of the region with the latest technical equipment.

We now go down Meteora Street and turn right into Ioanninon Street, which we follow until we reach the large crossroads at Pindou Street. Opposite, we see the town's wooded house hill ⓫, which we visit next. Just like the little church of Profitis Elias at the top, it is unspectacular, but in addition to reliable shade, it offers a beautiful view of the southern meteoric rocks and the entire south-eastern hinterland, even in the greatest summer heat. Low down, we see the open air cinema in the east and the third large church Agios Vasilios, also a new building, and in the south the stadium of the local sports club. There is hardly anything to see of the Pinios due to the lack of water.

We leave the Philosopher's Hill and stroll for a few minutes along the main artery, the Pindou or E 92. All the through traffic from north-central Greece to the west coast with the important port of Igoumenitsa passes through here. The traffic is correspondingly heavy at peak times. A large bypass east of the Pinios River is under construction, the route was mentioned in Route 9. From the railway station we turn left back to the centre.

The monasteries tour 'All Six'

On this 'classic' tour we want to see all six inhabited monasteries, at least from the outside. Theoretically, we could visit them all together only on weekends, because during the week at least one monastery is always closed for tourists. On the other hand, it would be a complete sensory overload to visit all the monasteries in one day. There is so much to see in each one, you also get to talk to monks and nuns - at least if it is not too crowded and you are really interested in the Orthodox religion.

So the best thing would be to consider this tour as a great meditative inspiration and visit one or the other monastery as a highlight. The choice is up to each person. After the author has visited each monastery almost a dozen times within two decades, the order is clear: all in first place! Each has its own special charm! All the monasteries were plundered and looted both during the Second World War and the subsequent Greek Civil War. They stood empty until the early 1960s, and from then on they were reoccupied and gradually restored. This work continues to this day.

If you want, you can walk the whole distance.

Alternatively, you can start by bus at Agios Nikolaos Anapavsas and end at Agios Stefanos.

From the centre of Kalabaka it takes about 35 minutes to reach the monastery of Nikolaos Anapavsas ❶ (see route 6). Many valuable manuscripts were found in this monastery. The paintings from 1527 and the frescoes in Cretan style are remarkable. Towards 1960, almost all the buildings had collapsed, after which they were restored. The small bell tower is particularly attractive.

From the monastery of Agios Nikolaos, we go up the asphalt road for a hundred metres and turn left onto the path to the monasteries of Metamorfosis and Varlaam (Route 6). At the fork, we turn left to Metamorfosis.

The monastery of Metamorfosis (Megalo Meteoro) ❷ was built in the middle of the 14th century on the highest and largest rock. Worth seeing are the frescoes in the main church, which was built in agiorite style (in the style of the Holy Mountain Athos) on a cruciform ground plan with a dodecagonal dome and lateral conchs. Impressive are the skull house (see p.21) with the skulls of the deceased monks as well as numerous buildings of various activities (wine barrel, farming implements).

From the Metamorfosis we walk down the road past the numerous buses and cars. At the bottom right we see the Varlaam monastery and cut down through a narrow path to the right.

Varlaam Monastery (also Agion Panton) ❸ used to be reached, like almost all other monasteries, by so called sky ladders or a net into which the monk allowed

himself to be pulled upwards. It was built in 1350. Apart from interesting fresco paintings, it has valuable manuscripts and religious treasures which can be seen in a museum. The refectory (dining room) and the kitchen are very well preserved.

From Varlaam Monastery, we go up to the right until we reach the descent to the Cat Church (route 2 opposite). At the asphalt road, we go left and shortly after the hairpin bend we come to the Rousanou Monastery.

The small but picturesque nunnery of Rousanou ❹ (also Agia Varvara) was built in 1545. The frescoes in the main church belong to the Cretan school. The small chapel was dedicated to Saint Barbara (Varvara). The fixed bridge that leads to the monastery was built in 1936. You can still see a long ladder on the building, which you had to climb up before.

Return to the hairpin bend and turn into the forest at the small 'car park' (Route 2 opposite) until you reach the ridge, then turn left to the shepherd's hut (Route 7). From the shepherd's hut we go to the monastery of Agia Triada and from there to Agios Stefanos, unfortunately on the road.

The monastery of Agia Triada ❺ was built in 1438 on the most picturesque rock. It has recent fresco paintings. A small chapel was hewn out of the rock.

The nunnery of Agios Stefanos ❻ was built in 1192. It can be seen from Kalabaka. It is also called the 'royal monastery' because an emperor was once a guest in the Middle Ages. Unfortunately, valuable wall paintings in the church were destroyed during the civil war.

The way back is either around St. Stephen's mountain (route 1) or the descent at Agia Triada (route 1 opposite).

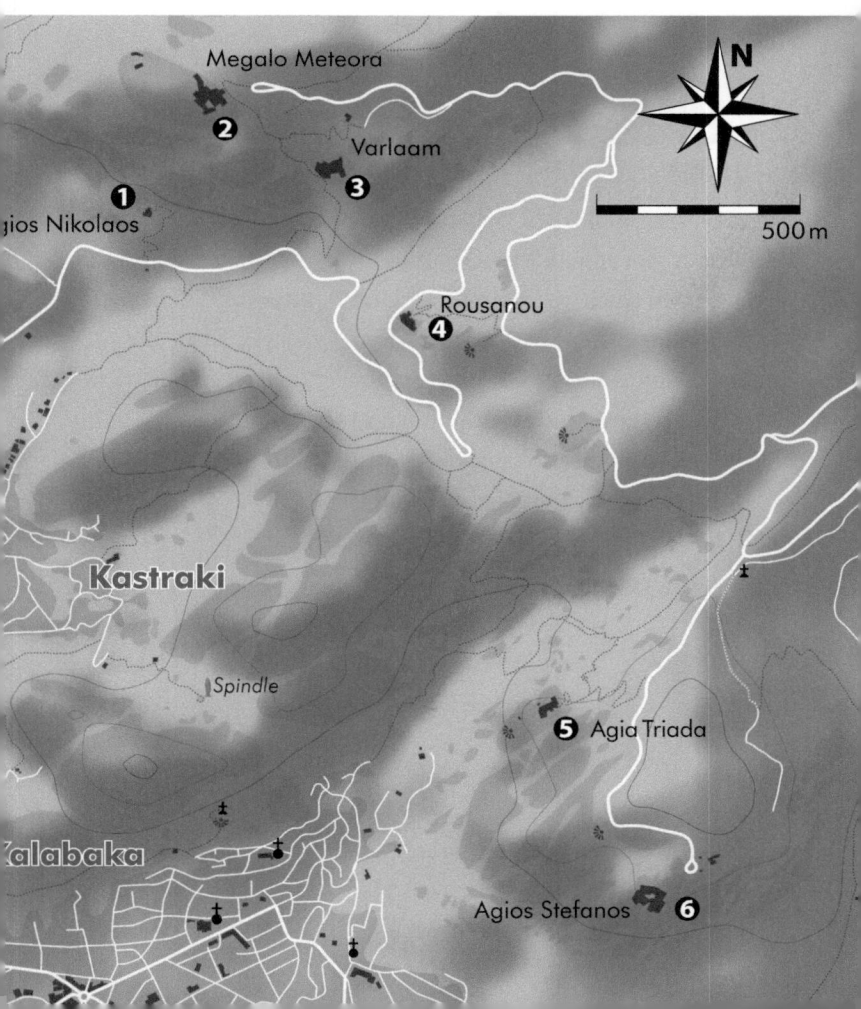

Additional information and tips

Further information about Meteora
can also be found under the following link:
https://www.salinos.de/links/meteora1.php

Meteora - between heaven and earth
The mountainous monastery landscape of Meteora between Kalabaka and Kastraki is a World Heritage Site.
It is visited by hundreds of thousands of people every year from near and far. Most of them travel to the monasteries by bus or car. This little booklet would like to invite you to dive deep into the world of Orthodoxy off the beaten track, to meditate and to pay attention to the little things along the way. An ancient tree, majestic storks on the church dome or the ruins of long-gone monasteries or hermitages - all these things want to tell us their story!

ISBN 9783746081243

Also available as a German version at:

'Meteora - zwischen Himmel und Erde'

ISBN 9783752804652

Info about the hiking maps
The maps published here (pp. 17, 22, 29, 35, 39, 45, 49, 55, 63, 71, 77) were created based on data from OpenStreetMap.org.
For copyright information, see www.openstreetmap.org/copyright.